Opening up Haggai

PETER WILLIAMS

DayOne

The Day One *Opening up the Bible* series is excellent for personal devotional use, but also very helpful for group study and sermon illustrations. You won't find deep expositions of the original Greek or Hebrew text but you will get straightforward, concise and practical overviews of Scripture.

Christian Marketplace Magazine

Although we know very little about the background of Haggai, there is no doubt about the central meaning of these thirty-eight verses. They were spoken (preached) between August and December 520 BC and were effective in stirring up the people to re-start their work on the rebuilding of the temple,

which was then in ruins. Such preaching, which leads to a positive response, is urgently needed today. Peter Williams' book is a helpful 'taster' for those who not only want to understand this prophecy but also desire to respond to it. May God bless and use *Opening up Haggai* to open up many hearts, minds—and pockets—for the service of God and his people today.

Michael Bentley

Retired pastor, Bible teacher, and author of several books

Dedication

My good friends Ruth and Brian Kerry have again given invaluable service in preparing this manuscript for publication and I am, as always, deeply grateful.

First printed 2008

ISBN 978-1-84625-144-3

British Library Cataloguing in Publication Data available

Published by Day One Publications

Ryelands Road, Leominster, England, HR6 8NZ

Telephone 01568 613 740 FAX 01568 611 473

email—sales@dayone.co.uk

web site—www.dayone.co.uk

North American email—usasales@dayone.co.uk

Printed by Gutenberg Press, Malta

Contents

List of Bible abbreviations

THE OLD TESTAMENT

Gen.	Genesis
Exod.	Exodus
Lev.	Leviticus
Num.	Numbers
Deut.	Deuteronomy
Josh.	Joshua
Judg.	Judges
Ruth	Ruth
1 Sam.	1 Samuel
2 Sam.	2 Samuel
1 Kings	1 Kings
2 Kings	2 Kings
1 Chr.	1 Chronicles
2 Chr.	2 Chronicles
Ezra	Ezra
Neh.	Nehemiah
Esth.	Esther
Job	Job
Ps.	Psalms
Prov.	Proverbs
Eccles.	Ecclesiastes
S.of S.	Song of Solomon
Isa.	Isaiah
Jer.	Jeremiah
Lam.	Lamentations
Ezek.	Ezekiel
Dan.	Daniel
Hosea	Hosea
Joel	Joel
Amos	Amos
Obad.	Obadiah
Jonah	Jonah
Micah	Micah
Nahum	Nahum
Hab.	Habakkuk
Zeph.	Zephaniah
Hag.	Haggai
Zech.	Zechariah
Mal.	Malachi

THE NEW TESTAMENT

Matt.	Matthew
Mark	Mark
Luke	Luke
John	John
Acts	Acts
Rom.	Romans
1 Cor.	1 Corinthians
2 Cor.	2 Corinthians
Gal.	Galatians
Eph.	Ephesians
Phil.	Philippians
Col.	Colossians
1 Thes.	1 Thessalonians
2 Thes.	2 Thessalonians
1 Tim.	1 Timothy
2 Tim.	2 Timothy
Titus	Titus
Philem.	Philemon
Heb.	Hebrews
James	James
1 Peter	1 Peter
2 Peter	2 Peter
1 John	1 John
2 John	2 John
3 John	3 John
Jude	Jude
Rev.	Revelation

Overview

What makes the book of Haggai especially interesting is that he was one of the three last prophets of the Old Testament period to receive God's revelation before the coming of Christ. He was a man with a single message for the people of his day, and he preached it with persuasive force and power.

That message was concentrated on the need to rebuild the temple, which had lain neglected for many years. But by the time Haggai appeared on the scene, the people had become dispirited and had lost interest in the rebuilding project. But he knew that its restoration was essential as the outward sign of the covenant, and of the Lord's presence with his people.

We know hardly anything about Haggai as an individual, but he must have been an inspiring preacher, for he succeeded in getting the people enthused for the work, and the temple was completed and dedicated in 516 BC.

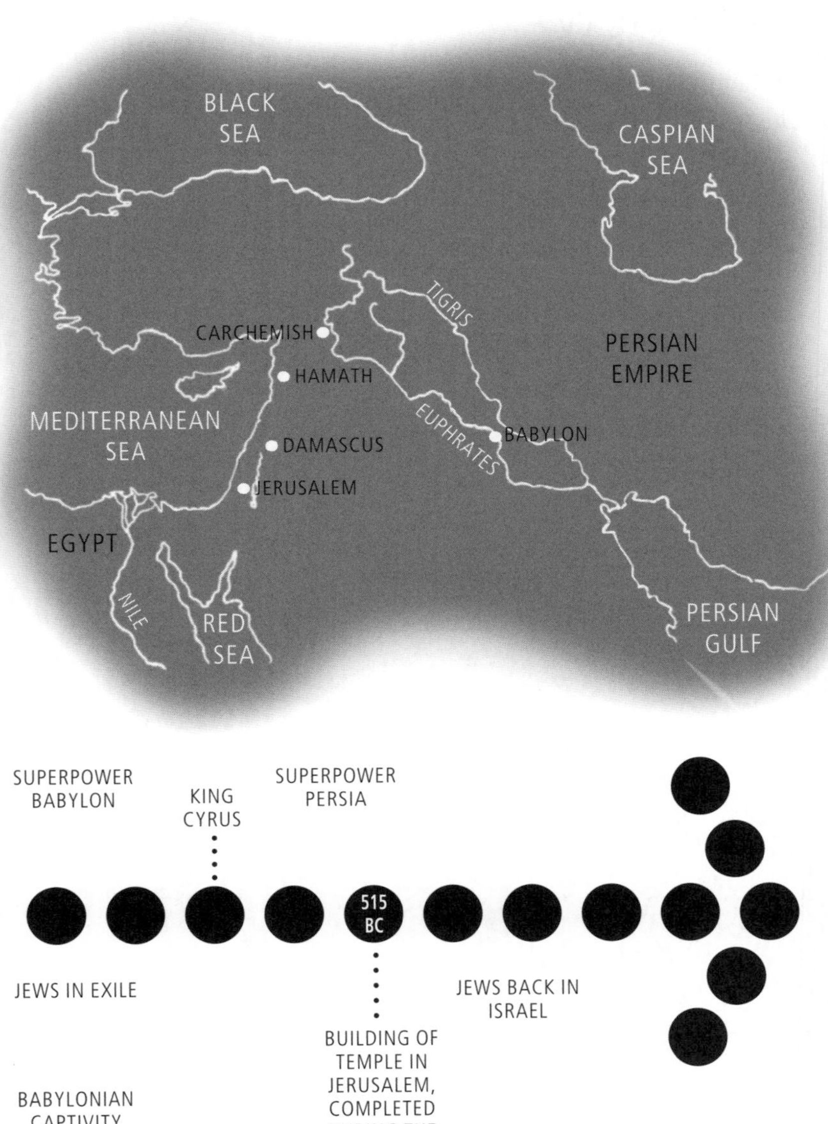
BLACK SEA
CASPIAN SEA
TIGRIS
CARCHEMISH
HAMATH
PERSIAN EMPIRE
MEDITERRANEAN SEA
EUPHRATES
BABYLON
DAMASCUS
JERUSALEM
EGYPT
NILE
RED SEA
PERSIAN GULF
SUPERPOWER BABYLON
KING CYRUS
SUPERPOWER PERSIA
515 BC
JEWS IN EXILE
JEWS BACK IN ISRAEL
BUILDING OF TEMPLE IN JERUSALEM, COMPLETED DURING THE REIGN OF DARIUS I
BABYLONIAN CAPTIVITY

Background

The book of Haggai belongs to that part of the Old Testament generally called the twelve books of the Minor Prophets. They are made up as follows: Hosea, Joel, Amos, Obadiah, Jonah, Micah, Nahum, Habakkuk, Zephaniah, Haggai, Zechariah, Malachi.

They are called Minor Prophets, not because they are less important in inspiration and reliability than the Major Prophets, Isaiah, Jeremiah, Ezekiel and Daniel, but mainly because they are shorter in length. Haggai is, in fact, the second shortest book in the Old Testament next to Obadiah, and comprises just two chapters. But although short in length it contains a powerful message which speaks to us today.

The events recorded are set within the context of the return of God's people from exile in Babylon, where they remained for seventy years as foretold by Jeremiah (Jer. 29:10). On their arrival back in Jerusalem, the exiles were met with a sorry sight. Their glorious city was in ruins, its walls heaps of rubble, and its beautiful temple a pile of blackened stones. But under their leaders, Zerubbabel and Joshua, the people—with enthusiasm and purpose—began the work of rebuilding the temple, but had succeeded only in laying the foundation when the work was stopped by command of the Persian king, Artaxerxes I (see Ezra 4:24).

For the next sixteen years, this situation remained unchanged and the foundation was overgrown with weeds. Then suddenly God raised up his servant the prophet Haggai, who, with his fellow prophet Zechariah, began his ministry of exhorting the leaders and the people to recommence the work of building God's house. But while the main message of the book centres on the rebuilding of the temple, it contains many other important lessons on obedience to God's word, the effect of powerful preaching, spiritual priorities, apathy and indifference, zeal for and worship in God's house, and the doctrine of the remnant.

As for Haggai himself, we know nothing about him apart from what we learn from his book, and from a couple of references in Ezra chapters 5 and 6, and Nehemiah chapter 8. His name means 'Festal' or 'Festive' and this suggests he might have been born during one of the great religious festivals in Israel. His prophetic ministry lasted only a few months from August to December in the year 520 BC. The book of Haggai is part of the final revelation of God under the Old Testament covenant before the coming of Christ in the New Testament.

There are three main characters mentioned in the book:

- Darius, King of the mighty Persian Empire, who ruled Judah from his capital in Babylon during the ministry of Haggai. He is also mentioned in Ezra 5 and Zechariah 1.
- Zerubbabel, the leader of the returning exiles from Babylon and the civil governor of Judah. His name means 'offspring of Babylon' and suggests that he was born in Babylon during the exile. He is also mentioned in Ezra 2:2 and Zechariah 4:6.
- Joshua, the High Priest, who was responsible for the spiritual life of the nation and shared the leadership with Zerubbabel. He is also mentioned in Ezra 2:2 and Zechariah 3:1.

ZERUBBABEL'S TEMPLE

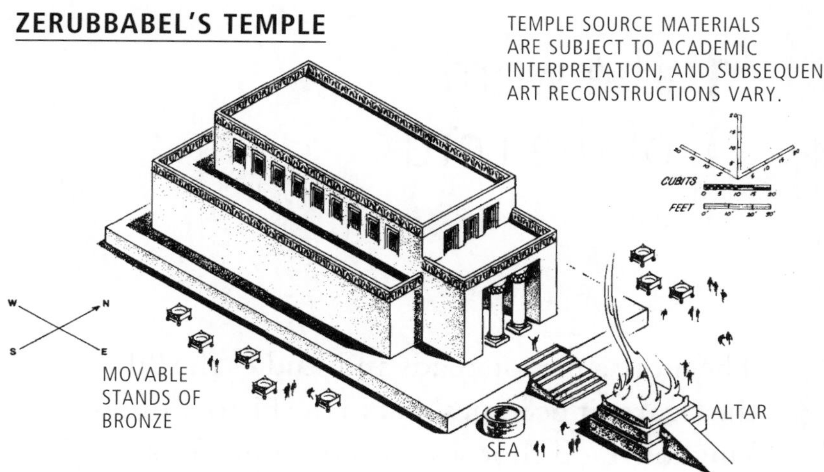

Construction of the second temple was started in 536 BC on the Solomonic foundations levelled half a century earlier by the Babylonians. People who remembered the richness of the earlier temple wept at the comparison (Ezra 3:12). Not until 516 BC, the 6th year of the Persian emperor Darius I (522–486), was the temple finally completed at the urging of Haggai and Zechariah (Ezra 6:13–15).

Archaeological evidence confirms that the Persian period in Palestine was a comparatively impoverished one in terms of material culture. Later Aramaic documents from Elephantine in Upper Egypt illustrate the official process of gaining permission to construct a Jewish place of worship, and the opposition engendered by the presence of various foes during this period.

Of the temple and its construction, little is known. Among the few contemporary buildings, the Persian palace at Lachish and the Tobiad monument at Iraq el-Amir may be compared in terms of technique.

Unlike the more famous structures razed in 586 BC and AD 70, the temple begun by Zerubbabel suffered no major hostile destruction, but was gradually repaired and reconstructed over a long period. Eventually it was replaced entirely by Herod's magnificent edifice.

1 The word of the Lord

(1:1)

The more a person reads and studies the Bible, the clearer it becomes that in the history of his kingdom God chooses special people for special tasks. Or, to put it another way, he always has the right man in the right place at the right time. That is one of the major lessons of Hebrews 11; that at certain strategic points in the history of the Old Testament God raised up Abel, Enoch, Noah, Abraham, Jacob, Joseph, and Moses; and in the New Testament, John the Baptist, Peter, Stephen, Paul and others; and in secular history, men like Augustine, Athanasius, Polycarp, Wycliffe, Tyndale, Luther, Calvin, John Knox, Whitefield, Wesley and others.

Haggai too was a strategic figure in the history of God's people. When he appeared on the scene in 520 BC, it was to be a turning point in the unfolding of God's purpose. Sixteen years had passed since the Jewish people had laid the foundation of God's house under the leadership of Zerubbabel and Jeshua (Ezra 3:7–13). In the meantime, the foundation had overgrown with weeds and the vision the people had once had of a renewed and glorious temple as the centre of worship had long since faded. Haggai's task when called of God was to rekindle that vision in the minds and hearts of the people and their leaders. That was an enormous challenge.

Haggai and the word of the Lord

'In the second year of King Darius, on the first day of the sixth month, the word of the LORD came through the prophet Haggai to Zerubbabel son of Shealtiel, governor of Judah, and to Joshua son of Jehozadak, the high priest' (Hag. 1:1).

The expression 'the word of the LORD' appears for the first time in the Bible in connection with Abraham in Genesis 15:1—'After this, the word of the LORD came to Abram in a vision'. Thereafter it occurs again and again in the Scriptures, especially in the prophetical books. It is an expression that reminds us of the great privilege that is ours when we are able so easily to hear the word of the Lord regularly in so many different ways.

There are still many parts of the world where people have not yet had the privilege and blessing of receiving God's word, whereas in the western world, we can hear it openly in preaching, through reading the Bible and Christian books, through audio and video recordings, and through services of worship on the radio and TV. But are we as appreciative of this as we might be? According to the Psalmist there is nothing in all creation to equal the privilege of having the eternal God communicate with us through his word. ‘For you have exalted above all things your name and your word’ (Ps. 138:2).

But if that is so, why is it that so many people in the western world today treat God’s word with total indifference and turn a deaf ear when it is preached? Particularly since at the same time they will listen readily enough to all those other voices in society trumpeting their messages of greed, or hate, or sexuality, or of violence through the mass media and the popular music of the day. Yet the word of the Lord has something terribly important to say about the really big issues of life and death, the forgiveness of sins and the promise of eternal life, but it fails to resonate with the man in the street.

Such deafness and insensibility to the word of the Lord would be incomprehensible were it not that the Bible itself gives the reason for it. There is a deadness and perversity within the human heart which makes it impossible, apart from God’s Spirit, for a person even to begin to appreciate what God is saying. Paul puts it like this: ‘The man without the Spirit does not accept the things that come from the spirit of God, for they are foolishness to him, and he cannot understand them, because they are spiritually discerned’ (1 Cor. 2:14). It is vitally important, therefore,

Such deafness and insensibility to the word of the Lord would be incomprehensible were it not that the Bible itself gives the reason for it.

that whenever we seek to bring the word of God to others, especially in preaching, we should pray that the Holy Spirit will authenticate the truth of that word to their hearts and minds and thus enable them to respond.

A personal word

Another thing to be noted in this verse is that the 'word of the LORD' came to Haggai personally. God singled him out from the crowd, as it were, and spoke directly to his heart and mind in the particular situation in which he found himself. It was as if God said to him, 'Haggai, I have a special word for your ears alone concerning the building of my house.' Not only does God have special men for special tasks, but he always has the right man, in the right place, at the right time. Well, that was certainly true of Haggai.

Consider the detailed timing given in this first verse regarding God's message. The word of the Lord came in 'the second year of King Darius, on the first day of the sixth month'—so the *time* was right. Similarly, the word came to 'the prophet Haggai'—so the *man* was right. And the word came to the prophet in Jerusalem of 'Judah'—so the *place* was right.

It is a wonderful experience and great blessing when the word of the Lord comes to us with the same personal directness with which it came to Haggai. For God still speaks out of his word in a personal way, and there is no doubt that many Christians have had that experience. For example, in my own ministry, in common with other pastors, I have had someone speak to me at the close of the service and say something like, 'That was a special word from the Lord for me this morning. I felt I was the only one in the congregation.'

And it may have happened to us in different ways. Perhaps we have been in the congregation when suddenly the word of the Lord through the preacher has taken on a special relevance and we have known without any doubt God was speaking to our personal situation. Or we may be reading the Bible or a Christian book, and a particular passage seems to leap from the page and we know God is speaking to us. Sometimes this happens when God speaks the word of salvation to a person's heart. The person may be listening to a sermon when suddenly he is overcome and convicted in his conscience, and knows that he has come to a critical point in his life and that God is calling him to repentance.

Isn't this precisely what happened on the Day of Pentecost? Peter had been preaching and then came the reaction of the people. 'When the people heard this, they were cut to the heart and said to Peter and the other apostles, "Brothers, what shall we do?" Peter replied, "Repent and be baptized, every one of you, in the name of Jesus Christ for the forgiveness of your sins"' (Acts 2:37–38). What had really happened on this occasion? Were the people responding in a positive way to Peter's eloquence and display of oratory? Of course not. The Holy Spirit was at work through Peter's preaching, authenticating it as the word of the Lord to the conscience of each of the three thousand people added to the church that day (Acts 2:41).

Receiving the word of the Lord

Another point worth noticing is that the first people to

receive the word of the Lord through Haggai were the civic and religious leaders. '… The word of the LORD came through the prophet Haggai to Zerubbabel … governor of Judah, and to Joshua … the high priest.' Furthermore, when they heard that word they accepted its divine authority. This is confirmed in verse 12: 'Then Zerubbabel son of Shealtiel, Joshua son of Jehozadak, the high priest, and the whole remnant of the people obeyed the voice of the LORD their God and the message of the prophet Haggai because the LORD their God had sent him.'

Clearly that tells us that the leaders and the people accepted the word of Haggai, not as his own opinion on the situation they were facing with regard to the building of God's house, but as a divine revelation. When it comes to the question of how we are to receive the word of the Lord, in a different context, the prophet Amos makes a point which has a direct bearing. '"The days are coming," declares the Sovereign LORD, "when I will send a famine through the land—not a famine of food or a thirst for water, but a famine of hearing the words of the LORD"' (Amos 8:11). We do not suffer from a famine of the word of God today, since we have the complete revelation of divine truth in the Bible. But there is certainly a famine of people 'hearing' the word of the Lord. And that is for two reasons.

First, people are not hearing the word of the Lord because in many pulpits the Bible itself is not being proclaimed as the authoritative word of God. Instead, it is being presented simply as the repository of people's thoughts about God, rather than God's thoughts about man. In this approach to the Bible, everything is to be questioned, rationalized, and explained in natural terms, including the great doctrines of creation, the virgin birth, the miracles of Jesus, his substitutionary death on the cross for our sins, and his resurrection. The result is that people are left in a state of utter confusion with regard to the church's message, since they are led to believe that the Bible can no longer be relied upon as the divinely inspired word of God.

If we want God to speak to us as clearly and positively as he did to Haggai, then we must open ourselves to the action of the Holy Spirit as we read the Scriptures or hear them expounded in a service of worship.

Second, even when the Bible is faithfully proclaimed, the fault for not hearing it as the word of the Lord can sometimes lie, not with the preacher, but with the members of the congregation. Writing to the Thessalonians, Paul makes this point: 'We also thank God continually because, when you received the word of God, which you heard from us, you accepted it not as the word of men, but as it actually is, the word of God, which is at work in you who believe' (1 Thes. 2:13).

It follows from what Paul is saying that people can hear the gospel when it is faithfully preached, and they can find it interesting, or intellectually stimulating, and even helpful and comforting if they are passing through a difficult time, but in no way does it authenticate itself to the mind and heart as the word of God. That is because they are hearing it only as 'the word of men'. Therefore they can leave at the close of the service doubting and questioning what they have heard because it has done nothing for the good of their souls.

If we want God to speak to us as clearly and positively as he did to Haggai, then we must open ourselves to the action of the Holy Spirit as we read the Scriptures or hear them expounded in a service of worship. For as long as we approach the Bible with the idea that it is merely a human record we shall never hear the authentic voice of God speaking to us from its pages—challenging us, and bringing us under its blessing or its judgement.

For further study ▶

FOR FURTHER STUDY

1. Read Exodus 3 and 4 for a long dialogue between God and Moses. Was Moses right to raise so many issues when God called him to lead his people out of Egypt?
2. Read Amos 8 concerning a 'famine of hearing the words of the LORD' and why it would happen. Read also 1 Samuel 3 where the word of the Lord was rare and there were not many visions, and see how God dealt with it by raising up Samuel.

TO THINK ABOUT AND DISCUSS

1. Do you agree that God has special people for special tasks? If so, try to think of one such person from the Bible, and one from history.
2. The work on God's house had been neglected for sixteen years. Were the leaders Zerubbabel and Joshua to blame for not rousing the people to action? And does this say anything about the responsibility of leadership in the church?
3. In the light of what we have said about the Bible as God's word, can you suggest a method for Bible reading that will help people to understand it better and to do it more often? What is your own method of Bible reading?
4. Have you had the experience of knowing that God has spoken to you personally, either in a sermon, or reading the Bible or a Christian book, or in conversation with someone? If so, tell others in the group about it.

2 Consider your ways

(1:2–11)

We saw from the opening verse of this chapter that the word of the Lord came to the prophet Haggai with a personal directness in the particular situation in which he found himself. That situation concerned the rebuilding of the temple, which had lain in ruins for the past sixteen years. In his message to the leaders and the people Haggai did some very straight talking.

The uselessness of excuses

'This is what the LORD Almighty says: "These people say, 'The time has not yet come for the LORD's house to be built'"' (Hag. 1:2).

Sixteen years earlier the people and their

leaders had set to work with great enthusiasm to rebuild God's house which had earlier been destroyed by Nebuchadnezzar. But then came opposition from the surrounding pagan nations and a decree from the emperor putting a stop to the work (Ezra 4). Gradually, the people's attention turned to their own private affairs, and they became used to worshipping among the ruins of the original temple. As the years passed, the vision they once had of God's house being gloriously renewed faded altogether, and if during the general conversation someone raised the issue by asking, 'Do you not think we ought to consider starting work on God's house?' the reply would be forthcoming, 'The time has not yet come for the LORD's house to be built.' And then they would trot out all the excuses why that was the case—lack of funds, shortage of materials, not enough craftsmen and so on.

It is a familiar story, isn't it? It's a matter of the uselessness of excuses, especially where God's work is concerned. It goes right back to the beginning of time with the fall of man in the Garden of Eden. 'The man said, "The woman you put here with me—she gave me some fruit from the tree, and I ate it."

'Then the LORD God said to the woman, "What is this you have done?"

'The woman said, "The serpent deceived me and I ate"' (Gen. 3:12–13).

Both the man and woman had enjoyed the freedom whether to eat the fruit or not, but neither was prepared to accept the responsibility that went with it. Adam blamed Eve, and Eve blamed the serpent. That is characteristic of life today. We live in a blame culture in which the fault is always elsewhere—with one's background, or a broken marriage, or lack of opportunity, or the management, or the people one works with. But never, it would seem, is one prepared to say, 'It is my fault, my sin, and I am responsible.' The sad thing is that this attitude is not confined to the people of the world, as is evident from this passage. Whatever excuses the people and their leaders made for their neglect of God's house, there was no getting away from the fact that they *were* God's covenant people, and the temple was the symbol of that covenant relationship.

An apathetic people

Although the people may have been scratching around for some reasonable excuse as to why the time was not right to start building God's house, the truth was that after sixteen years of inactivity, a spirit of apathy and indolence had crept into their thinking from which they simply could not rouse themselves. It was Haggai's intention to break through that inertia and get the people moving again.

Anyone with experience in leadership, especially in church life, will appreciate the enormous challenge facing the prophet. A lethargic, apathetic spirit, or that 'I cannot be bothered' feeling, is a dreadful thing to break, once it gets a grip on a person's mind and inclinations. It is like an insidious disease that erodes the will and destroys motivation. Today we are seeing a lot of that attitude in local church life. One growing sign of it is the gradual decline of the Sunday evening church service. And the blame for this cannot be laid wholly on the secularization of our day. It is largely the responsibility of Christians in the local church.

The most sinister aspect of an apathetic spirit in the

spiritual life is the manner in which it creeps up on us almost unawares. It is not as if we make a definite decision to stop attending the evening service, or the weekly prayer meeting, or to minimize the time given to Bible reading and private devotions. Rather, it is a spirit that, like a fog, stealthily and quietly envelops us until we lose our sense of direction in these things. And if something occurs to disturb our conscience and make us say to ourselves, 'It really is time I started attending evening worship again,' somehow—as for the people of Haggai's day—the time never does seem to be right, and the desire to move in that direction never really grabs us.

It all boils down in the end to a matter of personal discipline and a determined act of the will. Too many Christians are content with a flabby laid-back kind of Christianity, and do not give sufficient importance to the place of the will in the spiritual life. They seem to think that growth in grace happens automatically. It does not. One has to work at it! If we want to get our Christian life together, then we have to bring the will into action and put some effort and determination into it. When it came to building their own houses, the people of Judah were extremely active and showed plenty of determination and will-power. In her consecration hymn, Frances Ridley Havergal was so right to include the will in the gifts to lay on the altar for God.

Too many Christians seem to think that growth in grace happens automatically. It does not. One has to work at it!

Take my will and make it thine;
It shall be no longer mine.
Take my heart, it is thine own;
It shall be thy royal throne.

The wrong sense of priorities

When the people complained that the time was not right to start work on God's house, Haggai was all geared up with his answer. 'Then the word of the LORD came through the prophet Haggai: "Is it a time for you yourselves to be living in your panelled houses, while this house remains a ruin?"' (Hag. 1:3). And then he repeats the accusation in verse 9. '"You expected much, but see, it turned out to be little. What you brought home, I blew away. Why?" declares the LORD Almighty. "Because of my house, which remains a ruin, while each of you is busy with his own house."'

One can imagine the people and their leaders squirming with underlying feelings of guilt when Haggai confronted them head-on this way. For sixteen years the house of God was a heap of ruined stones, while they were preoccupied with refurbishing their own homes—in modern terms, adding the extension and the sun lounge, and building the patio and barbecue area. Haggai's accusation was a biting indictment of their inverted order of priorities as God's covenant people.

Now we must be clear that there was nothing intrinsically wrong with the people taking pride in making their homes comfortable, and in decorating them tastefully. That was perfectly in order. The trouble was that it had taken over their lives and had, to a certain extent, displaced the concerns of God's work in their order of priorities. They had plenty of vigour and energy to spend on their own life-style, but were tired and apathetic when it came to working on God's house.

From the Christian perspective, this question of priorities is a very important one. When our homes, families, work, pleasures, etc., begin to displace and jeopardize the centrality of Christ in our lives, it spells spiritual danger. It means we are beginning to live our Christian life at a shallower level, and that the Holy Spirit, instead of holding the controlling place, has to struggle and compete with all these other things to have so much as a foothold in our life. We then become like those people Jesus spoke of in his parable of the sower. 'Still others, like seed sown among thorns, hear the word; but the worries of this life, the deceitfulness of wealth and the desires for other things come in and choke the word, making it unfruitful' (Mark 4:18–19).

When it comes to having a right sense of priorities, John the Baptist has something to teach us. 'John wore clothing made of camel's hair, with a leather belt around his waist, and he ate locusts and wild honey' (Mark 1:6).

This is not to suggest that we live as primitively as John did. But clearly as God's man, his simple life-style was a living protest against much of the self-indulgence of his day. He had stripped life down to its essentials in order to live closer to God. And some of us could do with a bit of stripping down to a simpler life-style as Christians. If we are not careful, our lives can easily become so cluttered with secular interests and non-essentials that there is less and less time for the things that really matter, such as prayer, the reading of God's word, and meditation and worship.

A word of warning

Still with the question of priorities in mind, Haggai gives the people a serious word of warning.

> This is what the LORD Almighty says: 'Give careful thought to your ways ["Consider your ways", AV]. You have planted much, but have harvested little. You eat, but never have enough. You drink, but never have your fill. You put on clothes, but are not warm. You earn wages, only to put them in a purse with holes in it.'
>
> This is what the LORD Almighty says: 'Give careful thought to your ways. Go up into the mountains and bring down timber and build the house, so that I may take pleasure in it and be honoured,' says the LORD. 'You expected much, but see, it turned out to be little. What you brought home, I blew away. Why?' declares the LORD Almighty. 'Because of my house, which remains a ruin, while each of you is busy with his own house.'
>
> (Hag. 1:5–9)

This appeal to the people—'to give careful thought' to their ways, and take a good hard look at their life-style—was meant by God to be taken very seriously, for he repeats it twice more in chapter 2 verses 15 and 18. But what is God actually saying to them in this way? He is giving them a stern warning about getting their act together if they are not to experience his judgement and the withdrawal of his blessing. He reminds them that, as long as his house and his work remain neglected, they are losing out. He puts it like this:

> Therefore, because of you the heavens have withheld their dew and the earth its crops. I called for a drought on the fields and the mountains, on the grain, the new wine, the oil, and whatever the ground produces, on men and cattle, and on the labour of your hands.
>
> (Hag. 1:10–11)

God is saying in effect, 'Where has all this concentration and effort on your own life-style got you in the end? Are you any happier or more content? You give every moment to working in your fields to increase your income and standard of living—"You have planted much and harvested little". You are no better off; you still do not have enough food and drink to satisfy your hunger and thirst, or enough clothes to keep yourselves warm. And the little money you earn gets eaten up with inflation, like putting it into a bag with holes. And why is all this happening? Because you are neglecting my work and I am withholding my blessing. So you had better start thinking seriously about these things.'

What God is saying here may be applied in two ways:

First, it describes the feverish activity of our own age. People are living at a hectic pace without a thought for God, and are losing out as a result. There is an ugly itching discontent and covetousness at the heart of society. So many are obsessed with the pursuit of success and are working all hours to obtain it. Others are consumed with the glitzy life-style and the trinkets of modern consumerism. But is our society any happier? Is it not all a chasing after the wind? We are losing out in so many ways. Our children are losing out, our homes and marriages are losing out, and the lives of our young people are losing out through anti-social behaviour.

The quality of life as a whole is deteriorating. And our leaders and people in general would be wise to take God's warning seriously: 'Give careful thought to your ways.'

Second, we must apply what God is saying to the church today, because in some ways we are facing a crisis of faith. Many local churches seem to have lost their way, and are no longer secure in what they believe or what their role in society is. John Stott has expressed it thus:

> What is at stake is nothing less than the essential character of Christianity; is the Christian religion natural or supernatural? Various attempts are made to rid Christianity of its supernaturalism, to reconstruct it without its embarrassing miracles. But these efforts will be as fruitless as they are misguided. You cannot reconstruct something by first destroying it.
>
> Authentic Christianity—the Christianity of Christ and his apostles—is supernatural Christianity. It is not a tame and harmless ethic, consisting of a few moral platitudes, spiced with a dash of religion. It is rather a resurrection religion, a life lived by the power of God.
>
> (*Authentic Christianity*, Timothy Dudley-Smith, (ed.), IVP, p. 306)

Because the biblical message has been diluted, the church is losing out on God's blessing. And that blessing will not be recovered until the church recognizes that Christ governs the church through the word of Scripture. We need to give careful thought to our ways.

For further study ▶

FOR FURTHER STUDY

1. Read Ezra chapter 4 to see the context in which Haggai had to exhort the people to build God's house.
2. Read Jeremiah chapter 52 to learn how the temple was destroyed in the first place by Nebuchadnezzar.

TO THINK ABOUT AND DISCUSS

1. We live in a culture of blame-shifting. Would you agree with that statement? Are people today being encouraged to avoid responsibility for their actions? (Consider, for example, being able to sue the tobacco companies if one gets cancer through cigarette smoking.) What is the Christian view?
2. We are living in the day of 'small things' where the church is concerned. We no longer see big congregations, many conversions, or large numbers of children attending our churches. Are we losing out in the sense that God has withdrawn his blessing because the church is no longer faithful to the authority of the word of Scripture?
3. Do you think that evangelical Christians today could do with a simpler life-style? List what you think our priorities should be with reference to: financial giving; church attendance; hospitality; work in the church.

3 The remnant's response

(1:12–15)

In this third section of chapter 1 the leaders and the people respond to Haggai's preaching. 'Then Zerubbabel son of Shealtiel, Joshua son of Jehozadak, the high priest, and the whole remnant of the people obeyed the voice of the LORD their God and the message of the prophet Haggai, because the LORD their God had sent him. And the people feared the LORD' (Hag. 1:12).

Effective preaching

In verse 1 we noted something about the manner in which we are to receive the word of the Lord when it comes to us in a sermon, or in reading the Scriptures, or in a Christian book. In this section we see that under the preaching of Haggai, all the flimsy excuses the people had given for not getting on with the work of God's house were swept away as the word of the Lord got through to their hearts. It was effective preaching, and it persuaded them to respond in a positive manner.

Notice the phrases used to describe that preaching—they 'obeyed the voice of the LORD', 'the LORD their God had sent him', 'the people feared the LORD'. These are meaningful descriptions, which spell out the significance of preaching, and raise a very important question: What is it that makes preaching effective to the hearers? For there is no doubt that one of the most discouraging aspects of the Christian ministry is when the man in the pulpit prepares well and preaches his heart out, only to find that it has little or no effect upon the members of the congregation. And yet there are other times when things really do happen, the message strikes home to people's hearts and there is a positive response in renewing people's faith, or in conversions, or the reclaiming of backsliders.

> It sounds contradictory, but there is a sense in which effective preaching will be preaching in which the preacher is conscious of his own ineffectiveness.

A sermon has been described as being something that is 'thirty minutes to wake the dead'. That is not so far from the truth, because effective preaching is not only words, but is an activity, a deed, in which God himself is actively present by his Spirit, confronting men and women either to judge or to save. Eloquence and logical arrangement of material on the preacher's part are important ingredients, but it is not these that bring the message to people's hearts. It sounds contradictory, but there is a sense in which effective preaching will be preaching in which the preacher is conscious of his own ineffectiveness.

Think of Moses shrinking from the task of preaching to the Israelites in Egypt and telling God that they will not listen to him because he is slow of speech and tongue (Exod. 4:10). Or consider Jeremiah, when called to be a prophet, complaining: 'Ah, Sovereign LORD, ... I do not know how to speak; I am only a child' (Jer. 1:6). Even the apostle Paul, when reflecting on his own preaching ministry, exclaims: 'And who is equal to such a task?' (2 Cor. 2:16). And throughout history some of the most effective preachers have been those who confessed themselves bunglers to the end. John Knox, for example, ran out of the church at St Andrews in tears when called by the congregation to become their pastor!

Nor is it difficult to understand why there should be this sense of inadequacy when we consider the awesomeness of the preacher's task. He is not giving a lecture, or a moral address, but is preaching 'for a verdict' in relation to the destiny of people's souls. And no preacher is capable of obtaining such a verdict in and of himself. That is clear from Haggai's preaching. We are told that the people accepted his message 'because the LORD their God had sent him' (Hag. 1:12). That is saying that, while it was Haggai who did the preaching, it was God's voice the people were hearing. We understand the apostle Paul to be saying the same thing when, in answer to his own question 'Who is equal to such a task?' he says, 'but our competence comes from God [who] has made us competent as ministers of a new covenant' (2 Cor. 2:16 and 3:5–6).

God's remnant

Another insight into this passage focuses on the word 'remnant'. '… The whole remnant of the people obeyed the voice of the LORD their God' (Hag. 1:12). The same word occurs again in verse 14 and chapter 2:2. It is generally used of anything which is a small part of the whole, such as the last few yards left over from a bolt of cloth. But why should it be used to describe God's people in Judah?

Although the term 'remnant' is not always used, the teaching underlying it runs all through the Bible. It means that out of the mass of humanity God, through his free grace, always has a remnant who have accepted his salvation and who remain faithful to his truth at any stage in history. When Joseph was reconciled to his brothers in Egypt he said to them: 'God sent me ahead of you to preserve for you a remnant on earth and to save your lives by a great deliverance' (Gen. 45:7). When Elijah complained to God that he was the only one left who was faithful, God said, 'I reserve seven thousand [a remnant] in Israel—all whose knees have not bowed down to Baal and all whose mouths have not kissed him' (1 Kings 19:18). When speaking to those who will be saved out of Israel, Paul says, 'So too, at the present time there is a remnant chosen by grace' (Rom. 11:5).

The people of Judah are described as a remnant because they represented a tiny number who returned to Jerusalem out of the large number who originally went into exile. The vast majority had become used to a comfortable and prosperous life in Babylon and had no desire to undertake a journey of nine hundred miles to a Jerusalem that lay in ruins and a temple that no longer existed. In his moving prayer, Ezra, the leader of the returning exiles, refers to this fact. 'But now, for a brief moment, the LORD our God has been gracious in leaving us a remnant and giving us a firm place in his sanctuary' (Ezra 9:8).

The remnant today

The teaching on the remnant in the Bible has a twofold application for God's people today.

First, it speaks to the individual believer. In every age, however dark and spiritually barren, God will never leave himself without a witness. There will always be those who have been saved through his grace and who will remain faithful to his word. They may be small in number but they are to be found in remote mountain villages in China, and on the plains of Mongolia, as well as in large cities like Mumbai, Calcutta and Hong Kong. And in western nations, those of God's remnant are to be found in shops and offices, in factories and colleges—all who have not bowed down to modern Baals and the false gods of man's making. Being one of God's remnant can be a lonely undertaking on the university campus or in the place of work, but those who are faithful will one day receive the crown of life.

In every age, however dark and spiritually barren, God will never leave himself without a witness.

Second, the teaching on the remnant speaks to the church today. The general outlook for the spiritual life of places like Britain is bleak indeed when one considers how far removed from evangelical truth is the preaching and teaching ministry of so many churches. But that is by no means the whole story. There are still many churches, large and small, where the gospel is faithfully proclaimed, where the authority of God's Word the Bible is upheld, and where there is a zealous spirit in evangelizing and missionary work, and in reaching out to the community. These are God's remnant. And if and when God again visits such nations in revival power, it will be through these churches and not through the institutional church with its ecumenical structures and liberal theology.

The only question left to answer is one addressed to ourselves: 'Am I one of God's remnant today?'

Godly fear

We are also told in this passage that Haggai's message was accepted as God's message because 'the people feared the LORD'. The 'fear of the LORD' is something that is mentioned again and again in the Bible. Different expressions are used, such as 'reverence', 'awe', 'dread', and 'terror'. But they all denote essentially a holy fear that leads men to accept God's authority, and obey his commandments, and to hate every form of evil.

> Our fear of the Lord will not fill us with any sense of dread, but with delight and reverence in knowing and serving him.

If we ask the question of ourselves, 'Do we fear God?' we do not mean, 'Do we have a cringing fear of God's power?' but, 'Do we have a profound sense of God's holiness and mystery which leads us to worship him with reverence and awe in our souls?' It is significant that in the sevenfold gifts of the Spirit attributed to the coming Messiah, Isaiah says, 'He will delight in the fear of the LORD' (Isa. 11:3). As with the Lord Jesus, therefore, our fear of the Lord will not fill us with any sense of dread, but with delight and reverence in knowing and serving him.

Sad to say, this sense of awe in God's presence is often lacking in church worship today. Instead, in some forms of contemporary worship there is an easygoing familiarity with God that robs him of his majesty and greatness. This has meant in some areas of church life that the temper of Christianity has degenerated into a flabby humanitarianism, and in an age like ours when the church has its back to the wall, such a feeble view of God will never carry it to victory. We need, both as individual Christians and as a church, to revitalize our understanding of God as the One whom Isaiah saw in his vision in the temple.

> In the year that King Uzziah died, I saw the Lord seated on a throne, high and exalted, and the train of his robe filled the temple. Above him were seraphs, each with six wings: With two wings they covered their faces, with two they covered their feet, and with two they were flying. And they were calling to one another:
>
> 'Holy, holy, holy is the LORD Almighty;
> The whole earth is full of his glory.'
>
> (Isa. 6:1–3)

To fear God like that is to recognize the limitations of our humanity in the face of life's challenges, and our dependence upon him to overcome them. For the life of modern people is full of other fears—the fear of war, of redundancy, of losing one's pension, of old age and illness, of violence on the streets, of suicide bombers and of death. Job was so right therefore: 'The fear of the Lord—that is wisdom' (Job 28:28). If we feared God more, we would be wise enough to fear everything else less.

The stirring of the Spirit

In the last section of this chapter we have an instance of how God's Holy Spirit moves upon the human spirit through the faithful preaching of his word.

> Then Haggai, the LORD's messenger, gave this message of the LORD to the people: 'I am with you,' declares the LORD. So the LORD stirred up the spirit of Zerubbabel son of Shealtiel, governor of Judah, and the spirit of Joshua son of Jehozadak, the high priest, and the spirit of the whole remnant of the people. They came and began work on the house of the LORD Almighty, their God, on the twenty-fourth day of the sixth month in the second year of King Darius.
>
> (Hag. 1:13–15)

The message was brief, 'I am with you', but extremely powerful in stirring up the zeal of the people. It all happened in a mere twenty-three days, from the first day of the month (v. 1) to the twenty-fourth day of the month (v. 15). That is how quickly situations can change when the Spirit of God is present.

A Christian may be excused many things—a lack of intellectual ability, the lack of a great gift, the lack of fluency in speaking, or the lack of talent. But no Christian can be excused the lack of zeal for the cause of God, for that depends upon oneself. And without zeal, something vital is missing in a person's spiritual experience. When Jesus drove the moneychangers out of the temple, it is recorded that 'His disciples remembered that it is written, "Zeal for your house will consume me"' (John 2:17).

We can be consumed with zeal for many things in this life—our careers, our hobbies, our homes, our families, etc. But what we really need is for the Holy Spirit to stir up our spirit with an all-consuming zeal for the work of God and the gospel of our Lord and Saviour Jesus Christ. Amy Carmichael expresses it so well:

Give me the love that leads the way,
The faith that nothing can dismay,
The hope no disappointments tire,
The passion that will burn like fire;
Let me not sink to be a clod:
Make me Thy fuel, O Flame of God.

For further study ▶

FOR FURTHER STUDY

1. Read Job 28 where he asks the question: 'Where is wisdom to be found?', and answers it by saying: 'The fear of the Lord—that is wisdom' (v. 28). But in what sense is that true, and in what way does wisdom differ from knowledge?
2. Apart from the instances mentioned, try to find other passages in which the principle of the remnant is to be found. For example: 'God waited patiently in the days of Noah while the ark was being built. In it only a few people, eight in all, were saved' (1 Peter 3:20).

TO THINK ABOUT AND DISCUSS

1. Fear, awe, reverence, dread and terror: all these expressions are used in the Bible when speaking of our approach to God. Explain in your own words what you think they have in common, and where they are different.
2. Would you agree that certain forms of modern worship tend to trivialize God and rob him of his greatness? Give reasons for your answer.
3. How would you rate the following qualities needed in an effective preacher? Eloquence, clarity, sincerity, authority, intellectual ability, charisma.
4. Allowing for the work of the Holy Spirit, what steps could you suggest for stirring up a spirit of greater zeal in your church?

4 Past glory and present despondency

(2:1–5)

The first chapter ended with the people's zeal restored, and work on building God's house was begun on the twenty-fourth day of the sixth month (Hag. 1:15). But this chapter opens by telling us that less than a month later, on the twenty-first day of the seventh month, the situation had changed yet again. The spirit of zeal had evaporated, and had given way to an air of depression.

'On the twenty-first day of the seventh month, the word of the LORD came through the prophet Haggai: "Speak to Zerubbabel son of Shealtiel, governor of Judah, to Joshua son of Jehozadak, the high priest, and to the remnant of the people. Ask them, 'Who of you is left who saw this house in its former glory? How does it look to you now? Does it not seem to you like nothing?'"' (Hag. 2:1–3).

The problem stated

Why was Haggai led by God's Spirit to ask the people who could remember the first temple why they regarded the present building 'as nothing'? The fact was that among the older people, there were some who still recalled the magnificence and glory of Solomon's temple, and when they compared it with the present building, which was vastly inferior, they were filled with a sense of despondency and gloom which communicated itself to the rest of the people. We know this was so because the same thing happened sixteen years before, when the foundation of Zerubbabel's temple was first laid in the time of Ezra.

> And all the people gave a great shout of praise to the LORD, because the foundation of the house of the LORD was laid. But many of the older priests and Levites and family heads, who had seen the former temple, wept aloud when they saw the foundation of this temple being laid.
>
> (Ezra 3:11)

The fact was that Zerubbabel the governor simply did not have the resources to build a temple as glorious as that of Solomon, with its cedar panelling, and furnishings of gold and burnished bronze, and containing the Ark of the Covenant with its cherubim and mercy seat. That was the explanation for the people's mood of despondency. But they were wrong to feel that way, for the following reasons.

Externalizing religion

In the first place, they were giving an exaggerated importance to the external features in religion and worship. They were captivated by the memory of the magnificence of Solomon's temple and believed, in some strange way, that this was more glorifying to God than what went on inside it. But it is not the architecture and ornate interior of his house that pleases God in the first instance, but the reality of the worship for which it is intended. Consider the words of Jesus to the disciples when they expressed their admiration for the magnificence of Herod's temple.

> As he was leaving the temple, one of his disciples said to him, 'Look, Teacher! What massive stones! What magnificent buildings!'
>
> 'Do you see all these great buildings?' replied Jesus. 'Not one stone here will be left on another; every one will be thrown down.'
>
> (Mark 13:1–2)

In this way Jesus was not only predicting what would happen in the future, when Titus the Roman general would destroy the temple in AD 70, but he was also saying that its destruction was the consequence of the degraded worship that had made it the house of merchandise and a 'den of robbers' (Mark 11:16–17).

If we apply this to the British nation, it has to be said that we are famous for our magnificent cathedrals and beautiful old churches on which millons are spent for their preservation and restoration. But is God impressed with all this? This is an important question, especially if what goes on in many of them by way of worship is far removed from the clear preaching of the gospel for the saving of people's souls. Worship that is mainly concentrated on outward ritual in beautiful surroundings is empty religion without the reality and presence of the Holy Spirit in the hearts of the worshippers. This was the charge Stephen made against the Jewish authorities when he accused them of loving the temple building more than they loved God.

> But it was Solomon who built the house for him. However, the Most High does not live in houses made by men. As the prophet says:
>
> 'Heaven is my throne,
> and the earth is my footstool.
> What kind of house will you build for me?
> says the Lord.
> Or where will my resting place be?
> Has not my hands made all these things?'
>
> You stiff-necked people ... You always resist the Holy Spirit!
>
> (Acts 7:47–51)

Of course, none of this means that we are not to beautify God's house or show concern for dignity in the form of worship. But it does remind us not to elevate the externals of religion over and above the inwardness of our relationship with God. Otherwise we shall be like those Paul had in mind, whom he describes as 'having a form of godliness but denying its power' (2 Tim. 3:5).

Glorifying the past

The second mistake the people made was to idealize and glorify the past. But that was a wrong attitude. At this juncture they should have been praising God for their return from exile, and for the opportunity to rebuild his house and move forward to the next phase in the nation's history. We are all familiar with the 'good old days' syndrome, the tendency to look to the past through rose-coloured spectacles, and there was something of that with the people of Haggai's day. With wistful longing they wanted the pattern of the past repeated in their own time.

If we are perfectly honest, we can sometimes be guilty of the same thing. We look back to the great revivals of the past age of Wesley and Whitefield and the 18th-century Evangelical Awakening, and long for that pattern to be repeated when spiritual life today is so impoverished. Such longing is perfectly in order provided it inspires us in the present, and urges us to go forward with greater zeal in God's work. But the truth is that God's pattern in the past may not be his pattern for our day. We must not get despondent, therefore, because we do not see a repetition of past glory, or God's work in the present may well suffer.

God's pattern in the past may not be his pattern for our day.

The same is true in the life of the individual Christian. There are some who are always talking about what God has done for them in the past, and relating yesterday's experience. But the question must be: Is God using them and blessing them today? Are they moving on with God in Christ, and is their experience of God's salvation richer now than it was twenty or thirty years ago?

A false comparison

The third mistake the people made was to compare their present building with Solomon's temple. It was a false comparison because the circumstances in both instances were totally different. Solomon's was an age of economic prosperity and he had numerous building projects. It was said that 'silver [was] as common in Jerusalem as stones, and cedar as plentiful as sycamore-fig trees' (1 Kings 10:27). Zerubbabel, on the other hand, had come from exile to a land that had been decimated and had few resources from which to build the temple. But the important thing was that he used what he had.

In God's work we should not be looking over our shoulder at the work of others, and making unfavourable comparisons with our own.

The principle for us is that in God's work we should not be looking over our shoulder at the work of others, and making unfavourable comparisons with our own. For example, we may look at another church where the congregation is larger and where there are more conversions, and then we look at our own church where things are not nearly as exciting in spite of our hard work, and we become very despondent and depressed. Or we find ourselves looking at another Christian who is so wonderfully gifted and is 'up front' in the life of the church, and then comparing our own Christian life, which seems so low-key and insipid in comparison, and we get very discouraged.

The important thing in all this is to accept who and what we are with whichever gifts, great or small, God has given us, and to get on with his work in the situation in which he has set us.

A word of encouragement

We have seen how despondent the people were when they compared their own work on the temple with the glory of the first temple. What they needed, therefore, was a word of positive encouragement to lift their spirits and get them going again. And that is exactly what Haggai does in the second part of his message.

> 'But now be strong, O Zerubbabel,' declares the LORD. 'Be strong, O Joshua son of Jehozadak, the high priest. Be strong, all you people of the land,' declares the LORD, 'and work. For I am with you,' declares the LORD Almighty. 'This is what I covenanted with you when you came out of Egypt. And my Spirit remains among you. Do not fear.'
>
> (Hag. 2:4–5)

Notice the threefold repetition, the 'be strong' intended to emphasize the necessity and urgency to get on and finish the work they had begun. It is easy to begin anything, whether a building, or a project, or a particular calling, but to continue and finish it is the important thing. And that is true also of the Christian life. There are many who begin the Christian race, but for one reason or another become disillusioned and despondent and fall by the way. We should recall the words of Jesus: 'He who stands firm to the end will be saved' (Matt. 10:22).

Haggai does not exhort the people to be strong and continue the work in their own strength alone. He is aware of the difficulties they are facing, and to encourage them he says, '"For I am with you," declares the LORD Almighty. "... And my Spirit remains among you. Do not fear."'

That is the confidence we have in God's work, especially when we feel discouraged and are tempted to give up—God is with us and his Spirit indwells us, and we need have no fear that we will not carry it through to the end. As long as we hold on to that, nothing the devil might do to discourage and dissuade us will be successful. The apostle Paul puts it in his own unique way: 'Finally, be strong in the Lord and in his mighty power. Put on the full armour of God so that you can take your stand against the devil's schemes ... so that when the day of evil comes, you may be able to stand your ground' (Eph. 6:10–11, 13).

We all have our 'evil day' when the devil's attack is at its most ferocious and the temptation to give up is at its strongest, but if we are clad in the armour of God's presence, the victory will be ours.

FOR FURTHER STUDY

1. Read about the construction of Solomon's temple in 1 Kings 6–8, Zerubbabel's temple in Ezra chapter 3, and everything about Herod's temple in the Gospel accounts. Use a Bible dictionary and see what else you can find out.
2. Go through the Psalms and study those that deal with discouragement and how to handle it—for example, Psalm 73.

TO THINK ABOUT AND DISCUSS

1. Discuss the good reasons for looking back to the past, but also say why it is also at times negative and unproductive.
2. On a UK TV programme recently, viewers were told that one of the cathedrals had spent £10 million on the construction of a new tower. Was this good stewardship?
3. Do you believe that God can repeat the pattern of past revivals? Should we pray for that to happen again? Give biblical reasons for your answers.

5 The greater glory

(2:6–9)

The passage we are now entering is a complicated one, and it raises some very difficult questions about which Bible commentators are not always agreed. But it is also a very encouraging passage, for whereas the people had been looking back to the glory of the past, God now makes some wonderful promises about the future, and points them to a greater glory that is to come.

'This is what the LORD Almighty says: "In a little while I will once more shake the heavens and the earth, the sea and the dry land. I will shake all nations, and the desired of all nations will come, and I will fill this house with glory," says the LORD Almighty. "The silver is mine and the gold is mine," declares the LORD Almighty. "The glory of this present house will be greater than the glory of the former house," says the LORD

Almighty. "And in this place I will grant peace," declares the LORD Almighty' (Hag. 2:6–9).

Shaking the nations

God says that 'once more' he will 'shake all nations'. But what exactly does that mean? We know from Scripture that God had done some considerable shaking of the nations in the past when, for example, he brought the plagues on Egypt and destroyed Pharaoh's army in the Red Sea. He had also shaken and brought down the Babylonian Empire in order to bring back his people from exile. And here God says that he is going to do it once more, but it will not be a physical shaking of the heaven, land and sea by storms and earthquakes, but a shaking of the nations through political and social upheavals. God confirms this later through Haggai.

> Tell Zerubbabel governor of Judah that I will shake the heavens and the earth. I will overturn royal thrones and shatter the power of the foreign kingdoms. I will overthrow chariots and their drivers; horses and their riders will fall, each by the sword of his brother.
>
> (Hag. 2:21–22)

All these shakings and upheavals did in fact happen over the next five centuries up to the time of Christ. The Persian Empire, which had earlier conquered the Babylonian Empire and was the supreme power in the time of Zerubbabel, was itself eventually conquered and destroyed by the Greek Empire of Alexander the Great. But then Alexander's Empire in turn was destroyed by the mighty Roman Empire, which was the dominant power in New Testament times. These, therefore, were centuries of turmoil and warfare, of revolutions and counter-revolutions, all of which fulfilled what God had said: 'I will shake all nations.'

The shaking of the nations in the unfolding of history was all part of the preparation God was making for the coming of Christ and his gospel.

But what are we meant to learn from all this? It teaches us very clearly that God, in his sovereignty, uses the events in the rise and fall of nations to fulfil his own purpose in the world. The shaking of the nations in the unfolding of history was all part of the preparation God was making for the coming of Christ and his gospel. One has only to study the book of Acts to see in what way these disturbances on the world scene prepared the way for the spread of Christianity. Everywhere in Acts we see the influence of the Greek language and culture. For example, Paul's preaching throughout the Mediterranean world was in the Greek language, which by that time had become the common tongue. He was also helped in this because the Hebrew Bible had been translated into Greek before the time of Christ, which meant that both Jews and Gentiles throughout the Mediterranean could read it. Later, the New Testament itself was written in Greek.

The influence of Rome was equally important in preparing the way for the coming of Christianity. As well as being a Jew, Paul was also a Roman citizen, and Luke, the historian who wrote the book of Acts, shows how on occasions this was a great advantage in his missionary work (e.g. Acts 16:35–40). Moreover, the extensive system of Roman roads along which the legionnaires travelled made it easier for Christian preachers to move from place to place. And the Roman peace (*Pax Romana*, as it was called) ensured that sea travel throughout the Mediterranean was comparatively safe for Paul and his companions.

But the shaking of the nations is something God will do to an even greater degree with the coming of Christ and the winding up of history. The writer to the Hebrews refers to this by using this very quotation from Haggai.

> … but now he has promised, 'Once more I will shake not only the earth but also the heavens.' The words 'once more' indicate the removing of what can be shaken—that is, created things—so that what cannot be shaken may remain. Therefore, since we are receiving a kingdom that cannot be shaken, let us be thankful, and so worship God acceptably with reverence and awe, for our 'God is a consuming fire'.
>
> (Heb. 12:26–29)

The writer to the Hebrews is saying that everything and everyone not established in Christ's kingdom at the end time will be shaken and destroyed at the judgement. In Revelation, this final shaking is even more terrifying in the vision which describes the disintegration of the physical universe and of the whole fabric of society.

> I watched as he opened the sixth seal. There was a great earthquake. The sun turned black like sackcloth made of goat hair, the whole moon turned blood red, and the stars in the sky fell to earth, as late figs drop from a fig-tree when shaken by a strong wind, The sky receded like a scroll, rolling up, and every mountain and island was removed from its place.
>
> Then the kings of the earth, the princes, the generals, the

> rich, the mighty, and every slave and every free man hid in caves and among the rocks of the mountains. They called to the mountains and the rocks, 'Fall on us and hide us from the face of him who sits on the throne and from the wrath of the Lamb! For the great day of their wrath has come, and who can stand?'
>
> (Rev. 6:12–17)

The desired of the nations

Another expression about which Bible commentators disagree is the phrase, 'The desired of all nations will come.' There are three main interpretations given.

Some interpret it as a messianic expression referring to the coming of Christ into the world. Charles Wesley, in his well-known carol 'Hark the Herald Angels sing', understood it in this way:

> Come, Desire of nations come,
> Fix in us thy humble home.

But it can hardly be a reference to Christ since he never has been the desired of all the nations. On the contrary, he was despised by the world. Even his own Jewish nation rejected him: 'He came to that which was his own, but his own did not receive him' (John 1:11). And still today, Christ and his gospel are rejected by the nations of the world. Just think of the contempt and blasphemy heaped upon the Christian faith in Britain.

The second interpretation understands it to mean the desired 'things' of all the nations will come. This means that the Gentile nations will bring their riches into God's temple for God's work. This is thought to explain the mention of silver and gold in verse 8: '"The silver is mine and the gold is mine," declares the LORD Almighty.' But this need mean no more than that which God says to Zerubbabel—that he will provide all that is necessary for the building of his temple. We have the same thing in Psalm 50, where God says: 'for every animal of the forest is mine, and the cattle on a thousand hills ... for the world is mine, and all that is in it' (vv. 10, 12). After all, one of God's great names is Jehovah-Jireh ('The Lord Provides'—see Gen. 22).

In my view, the most acceptable interpretation is to read it as the desired 'people' of all the nations will come. That is to say, in every nation there are those who are desirable to Christ, for he has marked them out for salvation through his electing grace. This fits in much better with the context which speaks of God's glory: '"The desired of all nations will come, and I will fill this house with glory," says the LORD Almighty' (Hag. 2:7).

What could be more glorifying to God than to have people from all nations down through the ages coming into his house (temple) in response to the gospel? In Revelation it is written that 'with your blood you purchased men for God from every tribe and language and people and nation' (Rev. 5:9). This also links better with God's promise which follows.

The greater glory

'"The glory of this present house will be greater than the glory of the former house," says the LORD Almighty. "And in this place I will grant peace," declares the LORD Almighty' (Hag. 2:9).

Such a promise must have seemed unbelievable to the

people of Haggai's time, for they were still thinking of the outward glory of Solomon's temple. But the glory God spoke of would be greater because it would be spiritual, and not material like the magnificence of Solomon's temple with its cedar panelling and furnishings of gold and burnished bronze.

The truth was that the outward glory of Solomon's, Zerubbabel's, and Herod's temples was all eventually destroyed, and passed away. But the glory of those brought into salvation down through the ages would bring peace and reconciliation with God, and would last for all eternity.

FOR FURTHER STUDY

1. Read through Acts and look at the different instances where the influence of Rome, and Paul's Roman citizenship, helped the spreading of the gospel.
2. Read Revelation 8:6–13, 14:14–20 and 19:11–21 for further terrifying visions of the shaking of the nations in judgement at the end of time.

TO THINK ABOUT AND DISCUSS

1. The term 'glory' is difficult to define. What do you think is meant by the 'glory of God'?
2. Discuss the expression 'desired of the nations' and see if you can come up with an interpretation more satisfying than the three mentioned.
3. Does God intervene in history today? Discuss this in the light of the rise and fall of dictators like Hitler, Stalin, Milosevic, Saddam Hussein and others.

6 True holiness

(2:10–19)

Haggai's previous message was delivered on the twenty-first day of the seventh month (Hag. 2:1), when he encouraged the people to be strong and to continue with the building of God's temple.

Our present passage opens two months later, on the twenty-fourth day of the ninth month.

On the twenty-fourth day of the ninth month, in the second year of Darius, the word of the LORD came to the prophet Haggai: 'This is what the LORD Almighty says: "Ask the priests what the law says: If a person carries consecrated meat in the fold of his garment, and that fold touches some bread or stew, some wine, oil or other food, does it become consecrated?"'

The priests answered, 'No.'

Then Haggai said, 'If a person defiled by contact with a dead body touches one of these things, does it become defiled?'

'Yes,' the priests replied, 'it becomes defiled.'

Then Haggai said, 'So it is with this people and this nation

> in my sight,' declares the LORD. 'Whatever they do and whatever they offer there is defiled.'
>
> (Hag. 2:10–14)

This is a complicated passage and we need to think it through carefully if we are to grasp the point Haggai is making.

Holiness and defilement

Here is a kind of parable Haggai uses to show that it is always easier to spread spiritual pollution and defilement than it is to spread holiness and virtue. For example, if you take a glass of clean water and put into it a single drop of dirty water you will soon see the effect. But a single drop of clean water would have no visible effect.

Under the Old Testament law, if a priest were carrying consecrated (holy) meat from the temple sacrifice and it happened to touch some other food, it would not make that other food holy, for holiness cannot be communicated. But if a priest touched a dead body, he himself would be defiled, and everything else he touched would also be defiled (Num. 19:22). Haggai then applied these principles to the people. 'Then Haggai said, "So it is with this people and this nation in my sight," declares the LORD. "Whatever they do and whatever they offer there is defiled."'

God is saying that during the sixteen-year period when the temple was neglected, the people may have thought themselves holy because they were back in the Holy Land and the holy city, but in fact they were defiled because of their disobedience. The result was that everything they did was polluted—the harvests were poor and economic and commercial life had declined. God reminded them of this.

> 'Now give careful thought to this from this day on—consider how things were before one stone was laid on another in the LORD's temple. When anyone came to a heap of twenty measures, there were only ten. When anyone went to a wine vat to draw fifty measures, there were only twenty. I struck all the work of your hands with blight, mildew and hail, yet you did not turn to me,' declares the LORD. 'From this day on, from this twenty-fourth day of the ninth month, give careful thought to the day when the foundation of the LORD's temple was laid. ... Until now, the vine and the fig-tree, the pomegranate and the olive tree have not borne fruit. From this day on I will bless you.'
>
> (Hag. 2:15–19)

From the day the people sorted out their priorities and began work on God's house, they were showing true inward holiness and obedience to God's word, and he promised that they would experience his blessing in the future.

Now what are we to learn from all this? Here is how the principles underlying Haggai's parable apply to our own lives.

To defile is easy

The first principle states that to spread defilement and sinfulness is much easier than to spread holiness and virtue. Remember Haggai's illustration of the priest being polluted by touching a dead body and in turn polluting everything else he himself touches? Or remember our illustration of how

face and turn from their wicked ways, then will I hear from heaven and will forgive their sin and will heal their land.'

For further study ▶

FOR FURTHER STUDY

1. In the Old Testament, the Nazirite vow was a vow of holiness and separation to the Lord. Read about it in Numbers 6.

2. David's adultery with Bathsheba and his murder of Uriah lost him his sense of holiness and communion with God. The way back was slow and painful. Read 2 Samuel 12:10–11 and the following chapters up to 24 to see the troubles David experienced to the end of his life.

TO THINK ABOUT AND DISCUSS

1. Do you agree that it is easier to spread evil than holiness? Give examples. Also, how would you set about trying to bring another person into a holy life?

2. There is no such thing as instant holiness. The hymn writer says: 'Take time to be holy'. What are the things we should be doing to achieve this?

3. The underlying meaning of the word 'holy' is 'set apart for God and separated from the world'. Some have interpreted this as physical separation and have entered a monastery or nunnery. Do you agree with this? Give biblical reasons for your answer.

7 Zerubbabel—God's signet ring

(2:20–23)

In the final section of this chapter, Haggai receives a message from God which is directed personally to Zerubbabel, the civil governor of Judah.

'The word of the LORD came to Haggai a second time on the twenty-fourth day of the month: "Tell Zerubbabel governor of Judah that I will shake the heavens and the earth. I will overturn royal thrones and shatter the power of the foreign kingdoms. I will overthrow chariots and their drivers; horses and their riders will fall, each by the sword of his brother. 'On that day,' declares the LORD Almighty, 'I will take you, my servant Zerubbabel son of Shealtiel,' declares the LORD, 'and I will make you like my signet ring, for I have chosen you'"' (Hag. 2:20–23).

Zerubbabel God's man

Before we consider Haggai's message to Zerubbabel, we should first look at the man himself. He was certainly a very special individual, and he played a very important part in God's plan and purpose for his people. God says to him: 'I will make you like my signet ring, for I have chosen you.' In the ancient world, the signet ring was worn on the king's finger and carried the seal of his royal authority which was stamped on all official documents. (See Gen. 41:41–42.)

Zerubbabel, therefore, carried the divine authority on all that he said and did in the task of building God's temple. He was not a prophet like Haggai, or a priest like Joshua, but a statesman, and the civil leader of the Jewish community. It was under his leadership that the exiles returned to Jerusalem (Ezra 2:2), and he was entrusted with political authority as governor of Jerusalem by Cyrus the king of Persia. He came from the royal line of David, and his grandfather Jehoiachin was the next-to-last king of Judah (1 Chr. 3:17–19). He was also an ancestor of Jesus, therefore, and is mentioned in the genealogies of Matthew 1:12 and Luke 3:27.

Zerubbabel encouraged

Now consider the message. 'Tell Zerubbabel governor of Judah that I will shake the heavens and the earth. I will overturn royal thrones and shatter the power of foreign kingdoms. I will overthrow chariots and their drivers; horses and their riders will fall, each by the sword of his brother' (Hag. 2:21–22).

When the same message was given earlier through Haggai (see 2:6–7), it referred to the social and political upheavals that would occur in history down to the time of the coming of Christ and his gospel. But here the message is for Zerubbabel. But why did God say that? It was because Zerubbabel was living in difficult and dangerous times. We learn from Ezra that the surrounding pagan nations were the implacable enemies of the Jews and were determined by every means to prevent Zerubbabel from completing the work of building God's temple (Ezra 4:1–5).

The governor was in need of encouragement, therefore, and God—in the message of the shaking of the nations—gives him the assurance that he will keep him safe amid all the political upheavals of his own day, until his work is done. Zechariah, who prophesied alongside Haggai in Judah during this difficult time in building the temple, gave the same message of encouragement to Zerubbabel.

> This is the word of the LORD to Zerubbabel: 'Not by might nor by power, but by my Spirit,' says the LORD Almighty. 'What are you, O mighty mountain? Before Zerubbabel you will become level ground. Then he will bring out the capstone to shouts of "God bless it! God bless it!"'
>
> Then the word of the LORD came to me: 'The hands of Zerubbabel have laid the foundation of this temple; his hands will also complete it. Then you will know that the LORD Almighty has sent me to you.'
>
> (Zech. 4:6–9)

This message to Zerubbabel has a definite application to us as modern readers.

First, it tells us that in our work for God's kingdom we are not to rely on our own strength and power alone, but upon God's Spirit working through us. 'Not by might nor by power, but by my Spirit.' There is, of course, a place for human strength, planning and organization in the church's work, but it is God's Spirit coming upon his word who makes an impact on people's souls, reclaims backsliders, and energizes God's people for witness and service.

Second, it reminds us that we should not allow problems and difficulties, and the social and political upheavals of the day, to dishearten us and cause us to despair in God's work. God promised Zerubbabel that the mighty mountain (think of these as difficulties) would become level ground. Jesus used the same figurative speech to symbolize the obstacles encountered in the Christian life. '"Have faith in God," Jesus answered. "I tell you the truth, if anyone says to this mountain, 'Go, throw yourself into the sea,' and does not doubt in his heart but believes that what he says will happen, it will be done for him"' (Mark 11:22–23). Charles Wesley says the same thing in one of his many hymns:

Give me the faith which can remove
And sink the mountain to a plain;
Give me the childlike, praying love,
Which longs to build thy house again;
Thy love let it my heart o'erpower,
Let it my ransomed soul devour.

Third, this message tells us that what God begins he always finishes, including his work *in* us and *through* us. Speaking of our salvation, Paul says: 'He who began a good work in you will carry it on to completion until the day of Christ Jesus' (Phil. 1:6). And God says that 'the hands of Zerubbabel have laid the foundation of this temple; his hands will also complete it' (Zech. 4:9). He also says that Zerubbabel will bring out the capstone to complete the temple, and then there will be shouts of 'God bless it! God bless it!' (Zech. 4:7).

When the Lord Jesus died on the cross, his last words were:

'It is finished' (John 19:30). In the death of his Son, God was setting the capstone on the structure of his saving work, and we can shout from the bottom of our hearts: 'God bless it! God bless it!'

Zerubbabel the statesman

It has already been pointed out that, unlike many of God's servants in the Bible, Zerubbabel was not a prophet like Haggai, or a priest like Joshua, but a politician and civil leader. He was greatly honoured by God as his 'signet ring' and carried a special burden of responsibility as the governor of Jerusalem.

Throughout history, men and women in public and political life have been greatly used by God to further his purposes in the world. There are several instances in the Bible. Joseph was active in the political life of Egypt, holding the second-highest position next to Pharaoh, and was responsible for the agricultural policy that saved the nation from famine. Daniel held high office in the political life of Babylon, and served under kings Nebuchadnezzar, Belshazzar, Darius and Cyrus. Nehemiah, like Zerubbabel, was governor of Judah, and responsible for rebuilding the walls of the city. We ought not to be cynical, therefore, and think that being active in political life is incompatible with having a strong faith in God.

> We ought not to be cynical and think that being active in political life is incompatible with having a strong faith in God.

The truth is that we require more people like Joseph, Daniel, Nehemiah and Zerubbabel to take an active role in political and civil life. There is strong biblical warrant for that.

Both Jesus and Paul lay stress on the central place the civil authorities have in God's purpose for the world. When asked if taxes should be paid to Caesar, Jesus asked to see a coin, and, pointing to the portrait, said: 'Give to Caesar what is Caesar's and to God what is God's' (Mark 12:13–17). He meant simply that the state has rightful demands upon its citizens because it is ordained by God. Similarly, Paul says, 'Everyone must submit himself to the governing authorities, for there is no authority except that which God has established' (Rom. 13:1). He goes on to say that the state is God's servant and an agent of God's wrath for the punishment of wrong-doers.

The Scriptures also teach us that we should pray for godly men and women like Zerubbabel who carry the burden of leadership in public and political life. 'I urge, then, first of all, that requests, prayers, intercession and thanksgiving be made for everyone—for kings and all those in authority, that we may live peaceful and quiet lives in all godliness and holiness' (1 Tim. 2:1–2). For Christians, especially, we should pray that they will have the courage of their convictions in public life, and never be ashamed to own Christ as their Saviour and Lord.

FOR FURTHER STUDY

1. When Joseph was prime minister of Egypt, he had a definite agricultural policy for saving the country from famine. Read Genesis 41:33–49, 47:13–26.
2. Daniel was a great leader, but he made his first stand for God when only a boy of about seventeen years of age. Read Daniel 1.

TO THINK ABOUT AND DISCUSS

1. Do you think more Christians should be active in political life if they have the necessary gifts?
2. Scripture teaches that the Christian should submit to the authority of the state. But if the demands of the state conflict with the demands of the gospel, what then? For example, if you were living in a Communist state, how would this affect you?
3. What do you think are some of the qualities required in a leader? How could a leader in secular affairs develop and improve his or her skills and yet still maintain spiritual usefulness?

Opening up series

Title	Author	ISBN
Opening up 1 Corinthians	Derek Prime	978–1–84625–004–0
Opening up 1 Thessalonians	Tim Shenton	978–1–84625–031–6
Opening up 1 Timothy	Simon J Robinson	978–1–903087–69–5
Opening up 2 & 3 John	Terence Peter Crosby	978–1–84625–023–1
Opening up 2 Peter	Clive Anderson	978–1–84625–077–4
Opening up 2 Thessalonians	Ian McNaughton	978–1–84625–117–7
Opening up 2 Timothy	Peter Williams	978–1–84625–065–1
Opening up Amos	Michael Bentley	978–1–84625–041–5
Opening up Colossians & Philemon	Ian McNaughton	978–1–84625–016–3
Opening up Ecclesiastes	Jim Winter	978–1–903087–86–2
Opening up Exodus	Iain D Campbell	978–1–84625–029–3
Opening up Ezekiel's visions	Peter Jeffery	978–1–903087–66–4
Opening up Ezra	Peter Williams	978–1–84625–022–4
Opening up Hebrews	Philip Hacking	978–1–84625–042–2
Opening up Jonah	Paul Mackrell	978–1–84625–080–4
Opening up Joshua	Roger Ellsworth	978–1–84625–118–4
Opening up Judges	Simon J Robinson	978–1–84625–043–9
Opening up Luke's Gospel	Gavin Childress	978–1–84625–030–9
Opening up Malachi	Roger Ellsworth	978–1–84625–033–0
Opening up Matthew	Iain D Campbell	978–1–84625–116–0

Opening up Nahum	Clive Anderson	978–1–903087–74–9
Opening up Philippians	Roger Ellsworth	978–1–903087–64–0
Opening up Proverbs	Jim Newheiser	978–1–84625–110–8
Opening up Psalms	Roger Ellsworth	978–1–84625–005–7
Opening up Ruth	Jonathan Prime	978–1–84625–067–5
Opening up Titus	David Campbell	978–1–84625–079–8
Opening up Zephaniah	Michael Bentley	978–1–84625–111–5

About Day One:

Day One's threefold commitment:

- To be faithful to the Bible, God's inerrant, infallible Word;
- To be relevant to our modern generation;
- To be excellent in our publication standards.

I continue to be thankful for the publications of Day One. They are biblical; they have sound theology; and they are relative to the issues at hand. The material is condensed and manageable while, at the same time, being complete—a challenging balance to find. We are happy in our ministry to make use of these excellent publications.

JOHN MACARTHUR, PASTOR-TEACHER, GRACE COMMUNITY CHURCH, CALIFORNIA

It is a great encouragement to see Day One making such excellent progress. Their publications are always biblical, accessible and attractively produced, with no compromise on quality. Long may their progress continue and increase!

JOHN BLANCHARD, AUTHOR, EVANGELIST AND APOLOGIST

Visit our website for more information and to request a free catalogue of our books.

www.dayone.co.uk